ESCAPE TO REA   ...J, VOL. 1

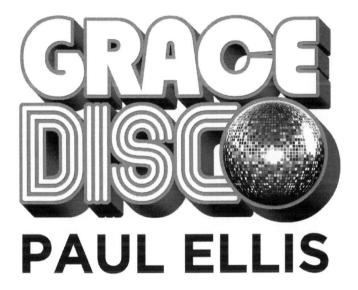

PAUL ELLIS

KINGSPRESS
Birkenhead, New Zealand

Grace Disco: Escape to Reality Greatest Hits, Volume 1

ISBN: 978-1-927230-21-3

Dedication: This is for all those passionate souls blogging about the goodness of God and his radical grace!

From E2R Readers

I had been searching the net for my intended sermon against "hyper-grace" theology. I found E2R and got convicted about mixing grace and works in my preaching for the last twenty years. Yes, I had read books on grace before but it was through the writings of Paul Ellis that God could finally reveal his true character to me. Since then something has changed in the deepest core of my identity. Shame got replaced with "I am the righteousness of God in Christ." What else has changed? Ask my wife!

- Reinhard L., pastor, Velbert, Germany

The intimidating gospel of our time left me crippled for over 30 years. Paul Ellis's message of grace has been the key to my freedom. I have now boldly stepped out into a missionary adventure carrying this message.

- José A., missionary, San Juan, Puerto Rico

I love E2R. I lived under legalistic and bondage teaching for many years. Then I happened to stumble upon E2R at the perfect time in my life. I get excited every time I see an E2R email in my inbox.

- Deborah L., cleaner, Hurdle Mills, NC

This may sound strange but reading new covenant messages on E2R made me feel like I've been born again *again*. Thank you Paul for re-introducing the gospel.

- Luis S.J., real estate broker, Malolos City, Philippines

Escape to Reality's presentation of the good news is so simple, even a twelve year-old could understand it. Paul Ellis's gospel is highly contagious and whole-heartedly recommended!

- Omotola O., software developer, Lagos, Nigeria

The Holy Spirit speaks through Paul Ellis' writing. How do I know? He has spoken to me. When I first encountered E2R, I'll admit I was wary; its message seemed too… appealing. But Jesus shone through the words and began to melt away my legalistic percep- tions. And then it was just me and him, and I finally grasped grace.

- Rachelle R., caregiver, Hunter Valley, Australia

When I came across the works of Paul Ellis I wanted to cry, jump around, and dance all at the same time. Finally someone else was speaking the pure, unadul- terated grace of our Lord Jesus. This is what the world needs to hear! This is what the world is hungry for!

- Tori C., college student, Spokane, WA

I found Escape to Reality after reading *The Gospel in Ten Words*. What an eye-opening view of the gospel and our heavenly Father! Now I understand that the gospel truly is Good News and I have a Father in hea- ven who loves me with an unending love no matter how badly I screw up here on earth!

- Anne G., bookkeeper, Chelsea, OK

Contents

A Word Before

For ten years I led a church in Hong Kong where I preached most Sundays. When we left Hong Kong and moved to New Zealand, I found myself without a pulpit but still with a burning desire to tell people the good news of God's grace. I began a newsletter which I emailed to my friends and that morphed into a blog called Escape to Reality, or E2R for short.

The blog went live on February 5, 2010 and received 20 visitors on its first day. Since then the blog has been viewed millions of times by people in virtually every country on earth. After five years I still find it amazing that a writer who lives in one of the most remote countries on earth can get a revelation from the Lord in the morning, put it on the web, and by lunch time have testimonies of how God used that word to set someone free in Norway or Nebraska or Novosibirsk.

Has the good news of God's love and grace ever travelled so far and fast so easily? Has there ever been a better time to be a good news herald?

Since E2R's fifth birthday is just around the corner, I thought it might be fun to re-release some of my favorite articles from the archives. Doing so would also give me an opportunity to polish them up and reflect on how they were written and received. Consequently, each article is followed by a brief "word after" where I share stories, memories, questions asked by readers, and that sort of thing.

Some of the material on E2R has gone on to shape chapters in my gospel books. However, for this collection of greatest hits I have drawn heavily on articles that have not been published anywhere else.

Why did I call this book *Grace Disco*? C.S. Lewis described our relationship with the Lord as a dance. If it is, it is not a ballroom dance that demands a high degree of skill, nor is it a ballet that requires years of training. Grace is a tune anyone can dance to. Grace is the happy beat that gets your feet tapping, your shoulders shimmying and draws you onto the floor.

School discos — remember them? They were great equalizers. On the dance floor it made not one jot of difference whether you were good at maths or were the captain of the team. All that mattered was that you joined in and had fun.

That's how it is with grace. It doesn't matter how good you are or whether you're some kind of big shot. All that matters is that you join in. And when you hear the sweet tunes of God's favor towards you, you will. You'll echo Mary who said:

I'm bursting with God-news; I'm dancing the song of my Savior God. God took one good look at me, and look what happened — I'm the most fortunate woman on earth! (Luke 1:46–48, MSG)

Dancing featured prominently in Jesus' life and stories and I think that's significant. Consider the prodigal son. That miserable excuse for a boy come homes, receives undeserved forgiveness and favor, and the next thing you know there's music and dancing (see Luke 15:25). It's like Jesus was trying to tell us that a good response to grace is to kick up your heels and dance.

And here's something you may not know about disco; it can literally save your life! I read that the American Heart Association uses the song "Stayin' Alive" to teach CPR to medical students. Apparently most people do emergency chest compressions too slowly. But the classic Bee Gees song, which featured in the 1977 dance movie *Saturday Night Fever*, offers close to the perfect rhythm. Now there's a tip to remember the next time you're faced with a life or death emergency.

The outrageously good news that Jesus revealed and Paul preached is the soundtrack of your new life. It's the song of joy that draws the wallflower out of the shadows. It is the life-thumping beat that raises the dead and rouses the weary. It's the tune of heaven that makes you dance and leap for joy!

1. Is God's Love Unconditional?

"How do you know God's love is unconditional? The phrase 'unconditional love' is not in the Bible." This is a fair question that cuts right to the heart of the grace message. Grace says that God loves us with no strings attached, but do a quick scan of the Bible and you will find that sometimes there *are* strings attached to the love of God. Or there seem to be.

Yet despite these few passages that say otherwise I am 100% convinced that God loves us unconditionally. You need to be 100% convinced too. So let me give you seven reasons for believing that God loves you unconditionally:

1. God's love is unconditional by definition

Different words for love are found in the Bible. *Agape*-love, which describes the character of God (see 1 John 4:16), is "unconditional, self-sacrificing, and active" love. The love of God is unconditional by definition.

If your experience of love is limited to what you have received from people, chances are you have encountered frail love that comes with expectations and baggage. But God's love is not like this for he loves you as you are and not as you should be. His love is unlike anything found in this world.

2. God's unconditional love is demonstrated on the cross

In Romans 5:8 Paul wrote, "God demonstrates his love for us in this: While we were still sinners, Christ died for us." God didn't wait for you to repent or confess or get cleaned up before he gave his life for you. The cross is the single greatest demonstration of unconditional love the world has ever seen.

3. God's love is immeasurable

In Ephesians 3:17–19 Paul dares us to grasp the width, length, and height of God's love. But you cannot grasp the extravagant dimensions of Christ's love — they are ungraspable.

Nevertheless Paul encourages us to "Test its length! Plumb the depths! Rise to the heights!" as Eugene Petersen says in the Message Bible, because if you had even the smallest glimpse of how much he loves you, you would be undone. Selfishness and clawing ambition would wither. You would cheerfully count your accomplishments and qualifications as rubbish compared to the awesome privilege of knowing Christ Jesus who loves you.

4. God's love keeps no record of wrongs

Jesus knew the name of every soldier who beat him, every mocker and hater, yet he still went to the cross so that they might be reconciled to God. It was as if God was not counting their sins against them! He wasn't, and neither is he counting yours (2 Corinthians 5:19). On the cross, justice had a meeting with unconditional love and your peace with God was secured. Your transgressions have been blotted out as if you'd never done them (Isaiah 43:25). Because God the Son bled for you, God the Father and God the Holy Spirit have both gone on record saying they will remember your sins no more (Hebrews 8:12, 10:17).

5. God's love endures — it never fails

> Love bears up under anything and everything that comes, is ever ready to believe the best of every person, its hopes are fadeless under all circumstances, and it endures everything [without weakening]. Love never fails [never fades out or becomes obsolete or comes to an end].
> (1 Corinthians 13:7–8a, AMP)

You can take the love of God and nail it to a cross and he will still love you enough to come back from the dead and hunt you down just to tell you that he's forgiven you and loves you and wants to be with you forever.

6. God's love is everlasting

Through the prophet the Lord says to us: "I have loved you with an everlasting love; I have drawn you with unfailing kindness" (Jeremiah 31:3).

7. God loves the unlovely

If you think God can't love you because of all the bad stuff you've done, consider those he loved in the Bible. He loved a murderer called David, a Pharisee called Saul, and when he walked the earth in human form he loved lepers, Gentiles, Samaritans, and tax-collectors. Have you ever wondered why?

God's love for us has nothing to do with our performance or our pedigree. It has nothing to do with our loveliness or worthiness. He simply loves us because *he is love* and it's his nature to love. And thank God this is so, for there is no hope *except* that he loves us with no strings attached.

If God did not love us unconditionally, he would not have died for us and there would be no covenant of grace. But he does and he did and there is! This is the good news the whole world needs to hear.

A word after

This was the first E2R article that was picked up and reproduced in a Christian magazine. I have mixed feelings about that. As a writer, I'm always pleased to have my work appear in traditional media outlets. But as a believer I'm staggered that 2000 years after the cross, Christians still need to be told that God loves them. Shouldn't this be old news by now?

Turns out some people get offended when you tell them that God loves them unconditionally. That doesn't sit well with what they've been taught.

Others like to have a bet each way. They say things like, "Sure, God's love is unconditional but…" before listing all sorts of qualifications and exceptions. It's unconditional love with conditions.

After writing the above article I was bombarded with questions like, "If God's love is unconditional, why isn't everyone saved?" or "If God's love is unconditional, why are people going to hell?" These are strange questions. You might as well ask, "If the sun is so hot, why am I so cold in the basement?"

My response to those who delight in debate and discussion is this: God loves you! If you can't see that—if that revelation doesn't burn in your heart putting everything else into proper perspective—look at creation, look at your kids, look at the cross. Your Father's heart radiates with molten love for you and he has been showing his love to you since the dawn of time. His love is like the sun—fierce and live-giving. If you haven't experienced the Father's love, the fault lies not with him. Step outside and look up!

Of course, not everyone is cool towards God's love. Many people told me that this article made them very happy. One reader said, "I no longer feel like I have to prove that I am saved by my works... I feel like a kid again." This youthful, joyful response is a normal reaction to grace. DIY religion and theological debates will make you feel old, but grace makes you feel young again.

2. God Doesn't Do Half-Jobs: Why Partial Forgiveness Is Completely Bogus

There's a teaching going around that says that God has only half-forgiven us. If that sounds wacky, that's because it is. But partial forgiveness is what you have if you think there are things you must do to stay forgiven. "Sure, Jesus forgave us at the cross, but to stay forgiven we need to forgive others or keep confessing sins or do other stuff." The implication is that if you fail to do these things, you fall out of God's mercy and forgiveness.

Three scriptures are usually offered in support of this teaching:

(1) Jesus said, "If you forgive other people when they sin against you, your heavenly Father will also forgive you" (Matthew 6:14), thus God's forgiveness is conditional on yours.

(2) Peter refers to being forgiven from our "past sins" (2 Peter 1:9), suggesting that your present and future sins are yet to be dealt with.

(3) John says you are cleansed only if you confess your sins (1 John 1:9), so if you don't confess, you're not forgiven.

Let's look at each in turn.

(1) Jesus said forgiveness was conditional

During the Sermon on the Mount, Jesus said we need to forgive others if we desire forgiveness ourselves. If you read this as a conditional statement—"You *must* forgive to be forgiven"—then you are reading it as a law.

Why did Jesus preach law? Because the Pharisees and legal experts had emptied the law of its power to silence the self-righteous. The law was intended to break our pride and reveal our need for a Savior. If you think the law is easy and do-able, you won't see your need for Jesus.

In the Sermon on the Mount Jesus declared that he had come to fulfill the law. He then proceeded to preach the perfect standard of God's holy law: "Be perfect as your heavenly Father is perfect" (Matthew 5:48).

How would you feel if the Sunday preacher said, "You must be perfect"? How would you respond if he said, "Unless your righteousness surpasses that of the Pharisees and the teachers of the law, you will certainly not enter the kingdom of heaven" (Matthew 5:20)? If your reaction is, "I'm in trouble, I need help," then you are closer to freedom than any Pharisee then or self-righteous person now.

The truth is the measure of forgiveness that we need from God is immeasurably greater than any

11

forgiveness we could show to others. But the good news is that Jesus fulfilled all the requirements of the law on our behalf when he went to the cross. In the very act of paying for the world's sin, he forgave us our sin. Do you see? The very condition for forgiveness that Jesus preached on the Mount, he himself satisfied on the cross. Now, in Christ, we have received the full extent of the Father's forgiveness.

(2) Peter implies that only our *past* sins are forgiven

When Jesus died on the cross he did not cry out, "It is half-finished." No, God doesn't do half-jobs. Everything that needed to be done to satisfy the demands of justice was done by Jesus. His sacrifice is the once and final solution for your sin (Hebrews 9:26). It's a simple truth, yet many people don't get it.

Peter writes that the reason why some Christians don't mature is that they have forgotten they have been cleansed from their past sins. Their knowledge of Jesus and what he accomplished is so limited that they live "ineffective and unproductive" lives.

You are a new creation. Your old sinful life is in the past. Although you may act like a sinner, you are a sinner no longer. Peter is basically saying, "Stop living in the past and grow up."

Paul wrote, "God made you alive with Christ. He forgave us all our sins" (Colossians 2:13). All means all. There is no sin Jesus didn't carry. There is nothing he didn't forgive.

You were forgiven 2,000 years ago. It's nonsense to say that God hasn't forgiven your future sins because when he forgave you all your sins were in the future.

(3) John says forgiveness depends on our confession

John writes that if we confess our sins he is faithful and just to purify us from all unrighteousness. Some take this to mean that we are cleansed through our confession. But John makes it clear that it is the "blood of Jesus" — not our confession — that "purifies us from all sin" (1 John 1:7).

Did you notice that John said "*all* sin"? Just in case you missed it, he says it again two verses later: Jesus cleanses us from "*all* unrighteousness" (1 John 1:9). All means all. All includes all past, present and future sin. When you are cleansed by Jesus you are well and truly cleansed!

> The Lord says, "Now, let's settle the matter. You are stained red with sin, but I will wash you as clean as snow. Although your stains are deep red, you will be as white as wool." (Isaiah 1:18, GNB)

John is not preaching human confession but divine forgiveness. Like every other writer in the New Testament he goes to great lengths to show us that forgiveness is a God-thing from start to finish. John writes so that you will confess or agree that God has done it all because only those who believe enjoy the blessings of God's great grace.

Some people try to put limits on God's forgiveness. They say that he withholds his forgiveness unless we do this or that or the other thing. They say that God forgives us in accordance with our behavior. But that is not what the Bible says.

> In him we have redemption through his blood, the forgiveness of sins, in accordance with the riches of God's grace. (Ephesians 1:7)

Just as you can't put a limit on the riches of God's grace, you can't put a limit on his forgiveness. Now *that's* good news!

A word after

If there was one drum that I bashed again and again in the early days of E2R, it was the subject of forgiveness. "You are forgiven. Period." For a while it seemed like I was writing about forgiveness every other week. I couldn't help myself.

14

Forgiveness is the front door into the House of Grace. If you can't grasp forgiveness, you won't grasp grace. This is just as true for believers as unbelievers, for there are many in the church who don't know they have been completely and eternally forgiven. They're trying to get forgiven or they're working to maintain their forgiveness. They're standing on the doorstep refusing to come in. "I just need to clean myself first." Good luck with that.

The bad news of dead works says "clean yourself first," but the good news of grace says "come as you are!"

3. Son, Servant or Friend of God?

How do you see yourself? As a (a) servant of God, (b) a friend of God, or (c) a son of God? To answer this question I ran a poll on E2R's Facebook page. To my astonishment, less than half of the respondents picked option (c). And so, once again, Facebook has answered one of life's great questions, which is this: Why is the world still a mess, even though Jesus did everything he came to do 2000 years ago?

The problem may not be what you think. It's not legalism, condemnation, or even sin. The root cause of the problem is that the majority of people do not see God as their Father. Like the prodigal, they relate to him as something other than sons. They have an orphan spirit.

There are only two kinds of people in the world: sons and orphans. Which are you? The devil likes to sow doubt by asking, "*If* you are the Son of God..." (Matthew 4:3). To the degree that you are uncertain about your sonship you have an orphan spirit.

I will probably write more about this some other time, but the FB poll has fired me up. I couldn't sleep for thinking about it.

I can't stay silent while some thief runs off with your birth certificates, so let me give you three reasons why (c) is the best response to the question above. Even if you serve a God who is your best friend, you are first and foremost a son, and this applies equally to the ladies, for we are all one in Christ.

The top three reasons why you are a son of God

1. The Holy Spirit says so. "God sent the Spirit of his Son into our lives crying out, 'Papa! Father!'" (Galatians 4:6, MSG). God himself calls you son. (You wouldn't want to call God a liar now would you?) He is the one who makes it possible for you to call him Papa.

2. The Bible says so in many places (see Galatians 3:26, Romans 8:14, Hebrews 12:7, and 1 John 3:1 for starters).

3. Jesus came to reveal the Father (Matthew 11:27). "Pray like this," said Jesus. "Our Father in heaven…" (Matthew 6:9). This is what makes the new covenant *new*. Sonship—not servanthood or friendship—is the pinnacle of redemption. How awesome is that?!

What are the benefits of sonship?

Someone with an orphan spirit may identify themselves as a servant of God. It sounds noble, but it actually insults the cross and the Spirit of grace. We are to be servant-hearted, not servant-minded. Do you know the difference?

A servant doesn't know his master's will, has to be told what to do, and relates to God on the basis of what he does. If he does good, he thinks God loves him more. How utterly tragic to live under such a lie.

A son is nothing like this for he has the mind of Christ (1 Corinthians 2:16), is clothed with his righteousness (Isaiah 61:10), and relates to God on the basis of the Father's love to him (1 John 4:19).

Servants suffer from performance-anxiety. Even friends may have to pound on doors in the middle of the night to borrow something (see Luke 11:5). But sons need never worry, for our "heavenly Father knows we need all these things" and he delights to give to those who ask him (Matthew 6:32, 7:11).

What about being God's friend? It's true that Abraham was known as a friend of God (Isaiah 41:8) and we are revealed to be friends when we do what Jesus says (John 15:14). This is a good thing and something to treasure. But sonship is better by far.

Sons have rights of access that servants and friends lack. Sons have an expectation of intimacy that servants and friends do not enjoy. My kids are with me 24/7 (it's the school holidays). In contrast, I only see and enjoy my friends occasionally. Wouldn't you rather enjoy God's presence continuously? As a son you have full rights to do so!

Finally, sons are heirs. All the cattle on all the hills and all the blessings of Abraham are yours, for we are co-heirs with Christ (Romans 8:17). Our share is no less than his!

What will it take to fix this broken, poisoned planet?

Answer: A revelation of the sons of God (Romans 8:19).

In the garden God gave us a planet to keep. We lost it, Jesus got it back, and yet we still act like it belongs to the devil. This planet is ours (see Psalm 115:16). Jesus paid a high price to redeem this planet for us. Creation is not waiting for God's servants or friends to rise up. Creation waits for his sons to rise up and say with authority, "This is my planet; hands off devil!"

If you're still having trouble wrapping your head around this, look to Jesus. Did Jesus describe God as his (a) Master, (b) Friend, or (c) Father? That's an easy question. Under the obsolete law covenant, God was Master. Under the Abrahamic covenant, God is our Friend. But under the new covenant God is revealed as our Father!

And don't water this down by saying that God is "all of the above." He's no more "all of the above" than you are "all of the above" to your children. My kids will serve many employers and have many friends, but they will only have one earthly father and that's me. I am thrilled beyond words to be identified as my children's father because it is my unique privilege. I hope they will be equally thrilled to be identified as my children. It makes my heart soar when they call me Daddy. I'm less thrilled when they call me "your majesty" or "boss".

God is your Father and my Father. Yes, I serve him and he is my closest friend. But service and friendship stem from my secure position as his adopted son. There's nothing I enjoy more than being with him, knowing him, walking with him, and talking with him. Every day with him is an adventure!

When you have a revelation of your sonship, it will change the way you pray. You will pray for the smallest things, because if it matters to you it matters to him. And you will ask for the big things, because God has promised you the nations. When you have needs, you won't hold back like a waiter or stand at a distance like a friend — you'll come running in to Papa knowing that he delights to give good gifts to his children.

A word after

You could say this article changed my life. About nine months after I started E2R, I began to realize that everything I write about grace is useless unless people see themselves as Christ sees them. Identity is everything. I didn't really get that before I wrote this.

When I discovered that many people are victims of identity theft—that is, they believe they are something other than God's children—I literally could not sleep at night on account of the burning desire to tell them the good news. "See the God that Jesus reveals. He's your Father who loves you as you are and not as you should be."

This article was the first of many that I would write about the believer's identity. It was the inspiration for an ebook called *Who's Your Daddy?* and it was the forerunner to my book *The Gospel in Ten Words*, which is all about our identity in Christ.

One of the things that has struck me since writing this is how deeply offensive the identity of sonship is to some people. Some would rather be known as God's servants than his children. One person told me, "I was created to serve." I beg to differ. This might surprise you but God doesn't need servants. Creation is not an expression of his desire for service or servants; it's an expression of his love. God wants a family!

"But what about when Paul calls himself a 'servant of Christ,' as he does in many of his letters?" I don't think the apostle of grace was any more confused about his identity than Jesus was when he referred to himself as the "Son of Man." Paul, along with every other New Testament writer, referred to God as a Father. He understood that we are the sons of God who serve people.

Jesus said he came to serve (Matthew 20:28) and those who follow him have the same heart. Jesus served the disciples and said "Follow my example" (John 13:15). We serve people in Jesus' Name. To say I am "a servant of Christ," as Paul does, means I serve with the same heart that Christ did, because his love motivates me.

4. God is Good But How Good Is He?

I read something on the weekend that hit me like a stone. It was written by someone who is troubled that the church no longer fears God like in the good ol' days of the Old Testament. The problem with the modern church, apparently, is we have "over-emphasized the goodness of God."

Think about that. We have *overemphasized* God's goodness. That's like saying, "God's good, but he's not *that* good. There's a tiny part of him that's bad."

I beg to differ. If I had just one adjective to describe God I would say he is love, but if I were given a second adjective I would say he is good.

Indeed, he is the very definition of good. Look up good in the dictionary and it says, "see God." Well, it should.

The devil—who is thoroughly bad—doesn't want us to think of God as being perfectly good. But he *is* good and everything he does is good.

The Jew says, "God is one," and he is.

The Muslim says, "God is great," and he is.

But the Christian says, "God is good" and the world rejoices!

It is the goodness of God that makes the good news good. Just as there is no bad news in the good news, there's no badness in God.

Imagine where we would be if God were bad, or half bad and half good. We would live under a cloud of uncertainty, fearful of his mood swings. But God is not like that.

God never has a bad day, nor even a bad moment. He doesn't have a bad temper. Everything about him is good and he is good all of the time.

All of his gifts are good. If you think you have found something good and it doesn't have God's fingerprints all over it, you are working with an inferior definition of good. God is the benchmark for what is good.

It is simply not possible to overemphasize the goodness of God. You might just as well try and over-emphasize his wisdom or try and grasp the breadth, width, and depth of his love!

God is good, all the time.

A word after

People sometimes ask me how I get the inspiration to write these articles. Honestly, it's not that hard. I don't see myself as doing anything other than stating the obvious in a world where the obvious has become buried under a lot of religious mumbo-jumbo. Anyone who knows Jesus can do it. You just have to believe that he is the first and last word on every subject.

For instance, if you hear that "God's goodness has been overemphasized," or "God gives and takes away," or "God's love is conditional," you need to ask yourself, "is this true in light of who Jesus is and what he has done?" Did Jesus ever seek to balance God's goodness? Did Jesus ever say God takes his gifts away? Did Jesus ever qualify the love of God?

After reading the above article a friend of mine called Gerry commented that God is so good that 1 Corinthians 15:33 — "Bad company corrupts good character" — can't touch him. I like that. All our badness cannot corrupt God's goodness. Indeed, the opposite is true. God's goodness is the ocean that swallows up our sin and corruption. He replaces our badness with his goodness and makes us new.

I guess that's why they call it *good* news.

5. How Well Did I Understand Grace Before I Understood Grace?

Have you ever seen those Magic Eye 3D pictures that look random at first glance but then reveal a hidden picture? There's a group of you looking and someone says, "Wow — look it's a ship!" Then another person sees it and now they're both describing the picture to you. But try as you might you just can't see it. They're pointing and saying, "Look — it's right there, with sails and everything. It's huge!" But you still can't see it. You're thinking there's no picture at all and they're deluded when suddenly, revelation comes and a ship appears. If you're like me and you're the last person to see these things, you'll embarrass yourself at this point by shouting, "I see it! I see it!"

That's how it was for me with grace.

I knew people who looked into the Bible and saw radical grace but I didn't. Sure, there were pockets of grace here and there, but there was a whole lot of other stuff as well. Then one day, revelation came and I saw Grace! He's right there on every page and in every book. How can you miss him? He's huge!

I now find myself reading old scriptures with new eyes and saying, "This is speaking of Jesus! This is all about him — I never saw this before." Now that I've seen him once I see him everywhere. I was saved decades ago and I have always loved God with my whole heart. But when I got this revelation of his amazing grace, it was like being born again, *again*.

A friend recently asked me, "How well did you understand grace before you understood grace?" (This question makes perfect sense to me.) Here's my answer: I thought I understood grace perfectly well. For as long as I can remember I've considered myself a testimony of his grace. But when Grace himself came into focus, I was floored. I realized that I had barely understood grace at all. Looking back I can identify nine signs that showed I did not fully grasp the radical and over-the-top grace of God.

1. I understood that I was *saved* by grace but not that I was *kept* by grace

I had received Christ by faith, but I was not continuing in that same faith (Colossians 2:6). Although I would never have said it, I had taken out a little works insurance. Faith is a positive response to what God has done, but I liked to initiate things and make things happen. Consequently, there was no rest, for there was always more to do. There was always another meeting to lead, another truth to teach, and another sheep to gather. I thought this was normal. I could get excited about the idea of being saved and saving others, but I was not drawing from the wells of salvation with joy (Isaiah 12:3). I was constantly

27

stressed and I treated grace as little more than grease for my engine of self-effort.

2. I felt obliged to serve

Jesus had done everything for me, what would I do for him? I didn't use the word "indebted" — that would've alerted me to the gracelessness of my thinking — but much of what I did was motivated by a sense of obligation. I thus cheapened the exceeding riches of his grace by trying to pay him back for his priceless gift. Inevitably this shifted my focus from him and his work to me and mine. Instead of being impressed by what Jesus had done, I was trying to impress him with what I was doing.

3. I motivated others using carrots and sticks

Because my own motives were screwed up it was inevitable that I would preach rewards and punishments. Do good, get good; do bad, get bad. I was preaching against legalism yet at the same time I was putting people under law! I was putting price tags on God's gracious gifts. I now realize that the moment you start charging for grace, even if it's the smallest, most reasonable fee, you've missed it.

4. I saw myself as a servant rather than a son

My identity was in the things I did rather than in my
Father. I saw myself as working *for* God (a noble
cause) rather than doing the works *of* God. I would
not have said I was justified by what I did for I knew
that grace and works don't mix. Yet I was mixing
grace with works like there was no tomorrow. And
here's the strange thing: Even though I preached
servanthood more than sonship, whenever there was
a crisis I was quick to relate to God as Papa. It was
only when I was strong and healthy that I was
seduced by my religious need to do something for
him. Happily, there were many crises!

5. I kept asking God to provide what he had already provided

I knew enough about grace to approach the throne of
grace boldly in my hour of need, but I didn't know
that God has already given us everything we need for
life and godliness (2 Peter 1:3). Like the prodigal's
older brother I felt that God would bless me as I did
my part. I didn't realize that I was already blessed,
deeply loved, and highly favored. In my ignorance I
wasted a whole lot of time doing a whole lot of nothing. I thought I was being active and fruitful, but in
reality I was passive and faithless.

6. I was more sin-conscious than Son-conscious

Like many Christians I was afraid of sin (keep it out of the camp!) and I was not known as a friend of sinners. I had read that the grace of God teaches us to say no to ungodliness, but I wasn't quite sure how that worked. So when preaching against sin I used inferior incentives like fear and punishment that led, at best, to temporary, flesh-powered changes in behavior. I emphasized *what we must do* (repent!) more than *what God has done* (forgiven us!). I kept the focus on us when it should've been on him and as a result my preaching was powerless and useless. If anyone failed to experience victory over sin, I figured they were unacquainted with God's transforming grace — even though I had given them none.

7. I always tried to do the right thing

Someone under grace says, "I trust him from start to finish. He will lead me in the right path." But in subtle ways I preferred rules to relationship. I craved Biblical guidelines for living. I thought I was choosing the good thing, but then so did Adam. We both had an independent spirit that led us to the wrong tree.

8. I had a stronger relationship with the written word than with the Living Word

I did not read the Bible to find Jesus but to answer the question, what should I do? I read indiscriminately and was often confused by scriptures that seemed to contradict each other. My solution was to go for balance: A little of this, a little of that, for all scripture is profitable. But by failing to filter what I read through the finished work of the cross, I unwittingly poisoned myself. I mixed the death-dealing words of the law with the life-giving words of grace. I thought I was zealous for the Lord, but in truth I was luke-warm. I was neither under the stone-cold ministry of the law nor walking in the white-hot heat of God's love and grace.

9. I knew I was righteous, but I didn't *feel* righteous

When I stumbled I would more readily confess my sins to God than allow the Holy Spirit to remind me of the gift of his righteousness. I knew I was a new creation, but in many ways I acted and spoke as though I was merely an *improved* creation. I thought honesty about my struggles was the key to getting more grace, but I probably would not have struggled so much in the first place if I had learned to see

31

myself as God sees me — as redeemed, righteous, and holy in Jesus.

Grace comes by revelation and if you don't yet see it then this article may sound like the ramblings of a man who is unbalanced. (Thank God I am. I'm done with balance!) But if you do see Grace, then right now you will be resonating like a tuning fork.

Let me finish with a few words for the non-seers: Please be patient with those of us who are leaping for joy. Don't walk away from the Magic Eye picture scowling, "I can't see it, there's nothing there." Just keep looking! Grace is standing right there in front of you and he's huge!

A word after

If I had a dollar for every time someone told me this article described their journey to grace, I'd have a lot of dollars. Perhaps more than anything I have written, this one resonated with readers who have experienced what I described as being born again *again*. I'm not talking about unbelievers getting saved. I'm talking about mature Christians who have found themselves dazzled by Jesus. I'm talking about people like Donna who told me, "These nine points describe my life as a believer for the past 18 years. I was blind but now I see!"

Another reader, Tracy, wrote this:

> Yes! Yes! Yes! I had been a Christian for over 25 years, and thought I understood Grace, but I never got it. Like you said, it's like these blinders have come off, and I want to cry that it took me so long to understand this. But I am also filled with crazy joy that I now do!

I like Tracy's emphatic affirmation because grace makes you shout "yes" to Jesus and all the promises of God:

> As surely as God is faithful, our message to you is not "Yes" and "No." For the Son of God, Jesus Christ, who was preached among you by us… was not "Yes" and "No," but in him it has always been "Yes." (2 Corinthians 1:18–19)

Someone who doesn't fully appreciate grace says "maybe," as in, "Maybe God loves me, maybe he's pleased with me, maybe I'll be counted as worthy." But someone who gets grace will always shout "Yes!" as in "Yes, I am righteous in Christ. Yes, God is pleased with me. Yes, Jesus loves me!"

6. The Top Twelve Blessings in the New Covenant

In Christ we get to partake in all of the blessings God promised to Abraham (Galatians 3:14,29). We also get all of the blessings promised under the law covenant and none of the curses (Galatians 3:13). This is really something when you consider the many blessings God offered in the Old Testament:

- To Abraham and his descendants God promised greatness, fruitfulness, great reward, world-reaching blessing, and more (see Genesis 12: 2–3, 15:1, 17:4–8, 22:18).
- To those who kept the law God promised long life, fruitfulness, abundant prosperity, protection, and more (Deuteronomy 28:3–13).

In addition to these wonderful promises, there are at least twelve awesome blessings God promises to us exclusively under his new covenant of grace. Here they are in no particular order:

1. God forgives all our sins (Matthew 26:28, Acts 13:38). Our sins are not merely covered by the blood of bulls and goats, they are carried and done away with by the Lamb of God (John 1:29).

2. God remembers our sins no more (Hebrews 8:12, 10:17). In terms of justification it's just as if we never did them.

3. God promises never to be angry with us again (Isaiah 54:8-9). Unlike the obsolete covenant of law, the new covenant is an everlasting covenant of love and peace (Isaiah 54:10, 55:3). God will never stop doing good to you (Jeremiah 32:40). Wow! Ruminate on that!

4. God qualifies us (Colossians 1:12). It's no longer a case of what we do (under the law covenant) or who we're related to (under the Abrahamic covenant). In the new, it's all about Jesus and what he has done for us.

5. God takes hold of us and never lets go (Philippians 3:12, Jude 24). Your security is not based on what you do but on what he's done and is now doing in you. Consequently, you can have confidence that he who began a good work in you will complete it (Philippians 1:6). Nothing can separate you from his love (Romans 8:39).

6. God blesses us with Christ's perfect righteousness (2 Corinthians 5:21). Righteousness is not some-

thing to earn, it is something to receive, and in him we have it (Romans 5:17).

7. God gives us the Holy Spirit to teach us all things and guide us into all truth (John 14:26, 16:13). We no longer need priests to mediate for us, for we can all know the Lord (Jeremiah 31:34). Indeed, we are his royal priests (1 Peter 2:9).

8. God is for us and not against us (Romans 8:31). God justifies us and there is now no more condemnation (Romans 8:1). When we sin, Jesus doesn't judge us, he defends us and empowers us to go and sin no more (1 John 2:1). He abundantly supplies all our needs so that we might enjoy life to the full (John 10:10, Philippians 4:19).

9. God is with us (Ezekiel 37:27). In the old, God's presence came and went, but in the new he has promised to never leave nor forsake us (Hebrews 13:5).

10. God empowers us to overcome the enemy (1 John 5:4). We have his delegated authority over demons and disease (Mark 16:17). Living under his divine protection and grace we are destined to reign in life (Romans 5:17).

11. God offers us his rest (Hebrews 4:10–11). Under the old covenant it was do, do, do, but under the new covenant it's done, done, done.

12. God gives us eternal life (Romans 6:23). Because Christ lives, we can truly live.

A word after

Those of you taking the museum tour will be interested to learn that this was one of the first lists I published on E2R. (I love lists.) It came out when E2R was about a month old. You can tell it's one of the early pieces because it's packed full with scripture references. Like a new preacher, I lacked confidence in my own voice and compensated by bombarding readers with scriptures. Sorry about that.

7. The Cure for Guilt

The other day I lost my temper. It was only for a moment, but it was enough. Damage was done.

Later, I felt sick about what I did and took steps to make amends. This is how guilt works. Guilt is a signal that our lives have been disrupted by sin. Guilt is a sign that a hurt needs to be healed.

But there's a problem. Ever since sin was given a free leash in the Garden of Eden, guilt has gotten out of control.

We feel guilty for things we did and didn't do. When we do well we feel guilty for not doing better. And when we fail, guilt pounds us.

Worst of all, guilt never goes away. Like an alarm that won't switch off, guilt is the soundtrack to our lives.

Burdened by guilt we may turn to religion in the search for relief only to be told that we're even worse than we thought. We have not only let down our friends and family, we've let down God.

With religious zeal we try to make the guilt go away but it's no use. We keep nine laws but break the tenth. We're good for six days but stumble on the seventh. No matter how hard we work, the guilt pile just keeps growing.

Guilt is a killer

I am convinced that guilt and condemnation are at the root of many of our health problems. Guilt breaks us. Our emotional bones were made soft for love, not hard for guilt-bearing.

I was a pastor for ten years and I can tell you that a lot of counseling done in the church is guilt-based. Pastors spend much of their time helping others manage their guilt. Which is ironic since pastors are often the ones making folk feel guilty in the first place. (Don't feel condemned my preaching brothers, but please stop preaching mixture. It's making people sick and sucking the life out of you.)

If only there was a cure for guilt. There is!

Let us draw near to God with a sincere heart and with the full assurance that faith brings, having our hearts sprinkled to cleanse us from a guilty conscience and having our bodies washed with pure water. (Hebrews 10:22)

Since the cross is God's cure for your sin, it is also his cure for your guilt. Do you battle with guilt? Do you struggle under the weight of your shortcomings and failings? Then look to the cross. Your sins are there not here.

Justified = not guilty

To be guilty means to be held responsible for your sin. I'm all for taking responsibility for our mistakes, but when it comes to sin all the responsibility in the world won't clear your sinful name. Your sin burden is too great.

But the good news is that Jesus took responsibility for all our sin. On the cross he literally became sin and in him sin was condemned (Romans 8:3). The gospel declares your sin problem has met its match in Jesus Christ. Do you know what this means? Under law, the best of us is justly charged *guilty* on account of sin, but under grace, the worst of us is justly charged *righteous* on account of Jesus.

This is one of the most profound revelations of grace yet many miss it. They say, "I know I am righteous and justified, but I still feel guilty." Connect the dots. If you are righteous and justified, you are *not guilty*.

"But, Paul, I feel guilty." That feeling is a symptom of unbelief in the goodness of God. Don't let that feeling run around in your head like a rat in the attic. Deal with it. Take that feeling and make it bow to the obedience of Jesus Christ.

He has forgiven you all your sins: Christ has utterly wiped out the damning evidence of broken laws and commandments which always hung over our heads, and has completely annulled it by nailing it over his own head on the cross. (Colossians 2:13–14, Phillips)

Under the law, there was a long list of charges against you. "You're a lazy Christian, a lousy parent, and a poor excuse for a human being." Do you know what Jesus did to those charges? He nailed them to the cross. That should tell you what Jesus thinks of all those miserable accusations.

Guilt from the Bible?

Many Christians battle with guilt because they've not fully grasped the finished work of the cross. They're filtering life through the obsolete lens of the rule-keeping covenant.

Guilt is what you get when you are constantly told that you are not *doing enough, giving enough, praying enough.* Since this mixed-up message is the predominant theme of graceless Christianity, is it any wonder that guilt has become an epidemic?

Much of what gets done in the name of the Lord is motivated by guilt. "Jesus died for you, what will you do for him?" You'd better get busy! "There are people going to hell because you are not evangelizing. Sign up for our outreach and make your guilt go away."

This sort of carry-on is appalling. It's manipulation of the worst kind and it is about as far from Jesus as you can get.

Making matters worse, many of our Bibles were translated by the guilt-conscious. Do you know how many times the words "guilt" and "guilty" appear in the New Testament? The answer depends on which Bible you're reading:

2	Young's Literal Translation
3	American Standard Version
6	King James Version
13	The Message Bible
15	New International Version
34	Good News Bible
45	Amplified Bible

What do these numbers mean? They reveal how much guilt is in your reading diet. For instance, if you read the NIV you're getting more than double the guilt that you'd get from the KJV. If you read the Amplified, you're getting nearly eight times the guilt.

Some Bibles should come with a health-warning: "Contains added guilt and traces of religious nuts."

I looked up all the Greek words for "guilt" and "guilty" in Vines Expository Dictionary and found there are actually very few. In fact, Vines spends more time listing words that have been *incorrectly* translated as guilty. I won't bore you with the details but here's an interesting question: Do you know how many verses say Christians are guilty? Answer: Zero. Nada. Not one. So the next time you hear a message that makes you feel guilty — that seeks to hold you accountable for something you've done or not done — you can reject it as unbiblical.

When I lost my temper the other day, I apologized and quickly made amends. There was nothing religious about that. It's just love. It's common sense. But works-based religion would have said, "Paul, you've not done enough. Every sin is a sin against God. On account of your sin you are now out of fellowship with him. You broke it, so you fix it. Examine your heart, confess your sin to God and he will wipe your slate clean."

Such a message appeals to our flesh but it's an anti-Christ pile of manure.

Instead of leading you back to the one you hurt, it'll cause you to withdraw and stare at your navel.

Instead of thanking God that in Christ you are always righteous, you'll waste time asking him to do what he's already done.

Instead of laying hold of the grace that empowers you to sin no more, you'll beat yourself up like a religious flagellant.

Learn the new language of grace

Guilt may be the *lingua franca* of dead religion but it wasn't a language the New Testament writers spoke. It's certainly not a language they speak in heaven. If you've been speaking the faithless language of guilt, I suggest you learn the new language of God's love and grace.

When you have seen the finished work of the cross it changes the way you look at your mistakes and failings. You no longer dwell on your weaknesses — there's no power there. Instead, you fix your eyes on Jesus who was "delivered over to death for our sins and was raised to life for our justification" (Romans 4:25).

When you sin, the accuser will seek to bring a case against you, and in the eyes of the law, he has a good case!

However, the issue is not whether you have stumbled but whether Jesus has been raised. If he has been raised then you have been justified. Case dismissed.

It takes no faith to look at your mistakes and condemn yourself.

It takes faith to look at Christ and say, "Because of you, I have been judged not guilty for all time. Thank you, Jesus!"

A word after

A couple of E2R readers raised some excellent points after reading this article. One observed that renewing your mind can be hard work. It's one thing for me to say, "change your thinking," but it's another to actually do that, particularly when you are battling against an old foe like guilt.

I appreciate that guilt is a big issue for many people and the last thing I want is to make people feel guilty for feeling guilty. However, if you struggle in this area, I want to encourage you to be quick to believe what God says about you. When guilt comes to condemn you, focus on Jesus and listen to him. Allow the Holy Spirit to convince you of your righteousness and agree with him. Tell yourself, "I am my Father's dearly loved child and I am the righteousness of God in Christ Jesus."

Another reader wrote to tell me that her feelings of guilt had little to do with unbelief in God's grace and everything to do with past hurts she had inflicted on others. This is understandable. God does not hold our sins against us but they still hurt real people. Some hurts can be mended; others cannot.

Sometimes we need divine wisdom to know how to respond to the damage we've done. In my case the remedy was obvious—I needed to apologize. But if the remedy is not obvious, perhaps because the hurts were inflicted long ago, I recommend you to talk to Daddy about it. Come boldly to his throne of grace and ask him what to do. He will show you the way to life and healing. He's pretty good at that.

8. Faith is a Rest

The gospel declares that God's grace comes to us through faith. So if you wanted to undermine the gospel, there are two ways you could do it: attack grace or attack faith. I usually talk about grace, but today I want to talk about faith because grace without faith is worthless:

> For indeed the gospel was preached to us as well as to them; but the word which they heard did not profit them, not being mixed with faith in those who heard it. (Hebrews 4:2, NKJV)

The gospel is true whether you believe it or not but it won't benefit you unless you believe it. If you don't believe Jesus has forgiven you, you won't walk in his forgiveness. And if you don't believe that in Christ you are already holy and acceptable, you will feel pressure to make yourself holy and acceptable.

Faith does not compel God to forgive us or sanctify us. Indeed, faith doesn't make God do anything. Rather, faith is a positive response to what God has said or done. Faith is acknowledging every good thing that is already ours in Christ (Philemon 1:6). Faith doesn't make things real that weren't real to begin with, but faith makes them real *to you*. For instance, if you battle with guilt and condemnation, you don't need Jesus to come and take away your sin. You need to believe that he already did. Jesus is the cure for guilt, but until you believe it, you won't be cured.

Faith is not a verb

Why am I saying this? Because there is a teaching going around that says, "Everyone is saved whether they believe it or not." Never mind that the apostles preached, "Believe and be saved" (Acts 16:31). Suddenly, encouraging people to "repent and believe the good news," as Jesus did, is politically incorrect. It's discrimination. It's putting barrier gates in front of the kingdom.

Perhaps you've heard something like this: "Believing is a work and grace and works don't mix." What a strange thing to say. It's like saying grace and faith don't mix or grace comes through unbelief. I wouldn't waste your time with this but I'm hearing it a lot. Maybe you are too. So how do we respond? What does the Bible say?

Now we who have believed enter that rest… (Hebrews 4:3)

Faith is not a work but is a rest. Faith is not a verb but a noun. Faith is a persuasion that God is who he says

48

he is, has done what he said he's done, and will do what he's promised to do. Consider Abraham, who…

> …did not waver through unbelief regarding the promise of God, but was strengthened in his faith and gave glory to God, being fully persuaded that God had power to do what he had promised. (Romans 4:20–21)

Faith is being fully persuaded. When you are fully persuaded, you can rest. The issue is settled, your mind is made up, and your heart is at ease.

We are creatures of persuasion. We are designed to operate from our convictions. Either you will be convinced that Jesus is true and good or you won't be. If you're not convinced the Holy Spirit will seek to convince you so that you can be persuaded and enter his rest. This is what the Holy Spirit does—he points us to the Prince of Peace so that we may find peace for our weary souls.

Unbelief is a work

When you have seen the beauty of Jesus, faith comes easily. Unbelief is the harder choice. To fold your arms and lock your jaw as the goodness of God assails you from every side requires real commitment.

Unbelief is not passive ignorance. Unbelief is hardening your heart to the manifest goodness of God. Unbelief is cursing that which God has blessed and hating that which he loves. Unbelief is resisting the Holy Spirit and clinging to worthless idols (Acts 7:51).

I am not talking about people who haven't heard the gospel. I'm talking about those who encountered the grace of God and rejected it. Instead of opening the door to the One who knocks (easy), they've locked it, pushed the chairs and table against it, and shuttered the windows (hard). Instead of reclining at the table of his abundance (easy), they're scrounging for food in the pig pen of independence (hard).

If faith is a rest, then unbelief is a work. Look at how unbelief is described in the New Testament and you will find plenty of verbs or action words. Unbelief is *rejecting* Jesus (John 3:36) and *denying* the Lord (Jude 1:4). It's *thrusting* away the word of God and *judging* yourself unworthy of life (Acts 13:46). It's *suppressing* the truth (Romans 1:18) and *delighting* in wickedness (2 Thessalonians 2:12). It's *turning* away (Hebrews 12:25), *going* astray (2 Peter 2:15), and *trampling* the Son of God underfoot (Hebrews 10:29).

And how does Jesus describe unbelievers? As evil*doers* and *workers* of iniquity (Matthew 7:23).

Do you see? It takes hard work to succeed as an unbeliever. You need to apply yourself with religious dedication. It's a life-time commitment with no days off. You cannot afford to drop your guard even for a moment or Jesus might sneak up and hug you. If faith is a rest, then unbelief is restlessness:

> And to whom did he swear that they shall not enter into his rest, except to those who did not believe? And we see that they were not able to enter in because of unbelief. (Hebrews 3:18–19, YLT)

Faith is a gift

There are two ways to get this faith-thing wrong: Tell people they must work to prove their faith or tell them they need no faith at all. The first is the message of graceless religion, the second is the message of faithless philosophy. In contrast to both, the gospel declares you need faith and God will provide it. Indeed, the good news of Jesus comes wrapped in faith (Romans 10:17). Unwrap the gift of grace and you will find it comes with piles of faith.

> Take my yoke upon you and learn from me, for I am gentle and humble in heart, and you will find rest for your souls. For my yoke is easy and my burden is light. (Matthew 11:29–30)

In a world of heavy burdens, Grace comes offering rest. Unbelief says, "Leave me alone, I'm busy." But faith responds, "Rest, you say? I'll have some of that, thank you very much!"

> For anyone who enters God's rest also rests from his own work, just as God did from his. Let us, therefore, make every effort to enter that rest... (Hebrews 4:10–11a)

Grace declares, "It is finished, the work is done," and faith responds, "Thank you, Jesus!"

The gospel is not an invitation to pick up tools, but to drop them. It's not a job advertisement; it's a day of rest.

Faith is not something you must do or manufacture. Faith is resting in the restful persuasion that God is at rest and in him so are we.

A word after

I'm not sure if I should say this, but this is one of my all-time favorite articles. Reading it now I feel so encouraged! In this world we face constant pressure to perform and produce, but whenever we hear the invitation to rest in Daddy's arms our souls melt with relief. It's what we were made for.

After reading this article someone asked me, "If faith is a gift of God, why doesn't he give this gift to everyone?" He does, or rather, he has.

We were all born with the need and desire for love, every single one of us. Since grace is an expression of love, we can say our desire for it is innate and God-given. God wants to supply our need so he gives us signposts — the air we breathe, the food we eat, the sunsets we enjoy, the friendship of others, his word, his Son — that all point to the love and grace of a good God. It's no special thing to be thankful for such things because we were made for such things.

The question is not why God only gives this desire to some, but why some walk with their eyes shut and their hearts closed to the abundant grace that surrounds them.

9. What is Biblical Confession?

Confession has become a touchy subject in the grace community. Judging by some of the comments I have received in the past week, there are some who think we must never confess sins, that to do so is to slap Jesus in the face and run back into performance-based Christianity.

It's true that confession has been abused. Confessing sins in an attempt to get God to forgive you is probably the number one work of the flesh. Yet confession can be good for you as we will see with six examples from the Bible.

What is the difference between good and bad confession? Biblical confession is declaring faith in God; bad confession is giving voice to unbelief. It is important that you understand this distinction.

True confession is agreeing with God, but bad confession is doubting him (e.g., asking him to do what he's already done, begging him to give what he's already given).

True confession leaves you Christ-conscious, but bad confession leaves you self-conscious.

To help you see the difference here are six examples of good confession:

1. Confession unto salvation

> But the tax collector stood at a distance. He would
> not even look up to heaven, but beat his breast
> and said, 'God, have mercy on me, a sinner.' I tell
> you that this man, rather than the other, went
> home justified before God. (Luke 18:13–14)

These seven words from the tax collector — "God,
have mercy on me, a sinner" — are the difference
between life and death, between justification and
condemnation. The tax collector is confessing his
need for mercy and he's looking to God to get it.

You don't need to beat your chest to get saved,
but you do need to put your faith in God and this
man does. Jesus says he went home justified. In other
words, he went home a new man and a sinner no
longer. The tax collector's prayer passes the test. It is a
good, life-saving confession. It is Romans 10:9 in
action.

2. Confession of sonship

> The Spirit you received does not make you slaves,
> so that you live in fear again; rather, the Spirit you
> received brought about your adoption to sonship.
> And by him we cry, "Abba, Father." (Romans 8:15)

If you have made the same confession as the tax collector there is no need to make it again. Once is enough. Don't go around telling people you are a "miserable sinner" or a "sinner saved by grace." If you've been born again, you are a sinner no more — you are a child of God. It's smart for sinners to confess like the tax collector and ask God for mercy and grace. But you do not need to ask for what you have already received.

The Holy Spirit in you cries out "Papa! Father!" (Galatians 4:6, MSG). Since true confession is agreeing with God, we too cry out "Abba, Father." As beloved children we don't stand at a distance beating our chests like the unsaved tax collector. We draw near addressing the Almighty One as "Daddy." True confession means seeing yourself as God sees you and he sees you as his dearly loved child.

3. Confession of sins

> Have mercy upon me, O God, according to your lovingkindness; according to the multitude of your tender mercies, blot out my transgressions. (Psalm 51:1, NKJV)

David had sinned and he knew it, yet he barely mentions his sin in this well-known Psalm of repentance. Instead he makes 24 statements about the goodness of God. This is significant. Under the law of the day, David deserved to die, yet in Psalm 51 he reminds himself of God's gracious nature—his lovingkindness and tender mercies. Since this Psalm is full of faith in the goodness of God, it passes the confession test.

It's good to be open and honest about our mistakes, but when you sin take your cue from David. Don't stare at your navel but lift your eyes to heaven and praise God for his goodness and mercy. Thank him that all your sins were taken away at the cross and that because of Jesus you are a sinner no more.

When you sin it takes no faith to confess your guilt and shame; it takes faith to look to the cross and declare, "Because of his grace I am still forgiven, I am still righteous, I am still a child of God. Thank you, Jesus!"

4. Confession in times of suffering

He said to them, "I am so sad that I feel as if I am dying. Stay here and keep awake with me." Jesus walked on a little way. Then he knelt with his face to the ground and prayed, "My Father, if it is possible, don't make me suffer by having me drink from this cup. But do what you want, and not what I want." (Matthew 26:38–39, CEV)

Jesus' greatest hour of need was in the Garden of Gethsemane. His soul was crushed with the weight of the world. Did Jesus put on a mask and pretend he had it altogether? No. He opened his mouth and confessed with honest transparency.

Confession is not just for sin, it's for our sufferings as well. If you're going through a rough patch, be encouraged by Jesus. He was so stressed, he sweated blood! Everyone gets stressed; it's what you do when you're stressed that makes the difference. What did Jesus do? He presented his requests to God but did so in a way that expressed his faith in God's goodness.

It's like he was saying, "I don't know if I can go through with this Father, but I trust you." Do you see? Honesty ("I'm dying here!") plus faith ("your will be done") helps us receive grace in our hour of need.

If you're in an environment that places a big emphasis on walking in victory every day, you need to hear this: unless you are honest and open about your needs, you will never receive the grace that propels us through life's trials. Grace is for the needy and we are all needy. We're just not all honest about it.

5. Confession and sickness

As Jesus went on from there, two blind men followed him, calling out, "Have mercy on us, Son of David!" When he had gone indoors, the blind men came to him, and he asked them, "Do you believe that I am able to do this?" "Yes, Lord," they replied. Then he touched their eyes and said, "According to your faith will it be done to you"; and their sight was restored. (Matthew 9:27–30a)

I guess there were many blind men in Israel but these two opened their mouths and confessed their need to Jesus. Look at what Jesus asked them. "Do you believe?" It's like Jesus was on a faith-hunt. I'm sure Jesus could sense the faith in their hearts but he wanted them to speak it out. It's as if they needed to hear their own good confession. "Yes, Lord, we believe." Any time you say "Yes" to Jesus, that's a good confession. It's giving voice to the faith in your heart.

I speak to sicknesses all the time. I tell them about Jesus by whose stripes we are healed. I command them to bow to King Jesus and they often do. Not everyone I pray for gets healed, but more people get healed when I confess the name of Jesus than when I stay silent.

So far we have seen that a confession can be helpful when dealing with salvation, sonship, sin, suffering, and sickness. There is one more occasion when confession is good.

6. Confession as a sacrifice

> Through Jesus, therefore, let us continually offer
> to God a sacrifice of praise—the fruit of lips that
> confess his name. (Hebrews 13:15)

The word for confess here is exactly the same as the
word for confess in 1 John 1:9 and elsewhere and it
means to agree with God. Every time we praise God
for his goodness and mercy, we are making a good
confession.

The writer of Hebrews says this is to be our habit.
You may be locked up in prison like Paul and Silas—
praise him anyway, for he is good. Your life may be
going down the toilet, but guess what—God is still
good.

Instead of giving voice to the trials of your life,
speak to your storms about the goodness of your
good God. Rebuke your problems, resist the devil,
bless those who curse you, pray for your enemies and
fight the good fight.

Gratitude is the language of faith. Anytime you
give thanks to God, you are making a good confession. Want to be a good confessor? Then learn to
give thanks in all circumstances (1 Thessalonians
5:18).

True confession = "Jesus!"

True confession is basically proclaiming Jesus over our lives. It is declaring the good news of his kingdom, it is proclaiming the gospel of his grace, and it is saying "Thank you, Lord!"

The devil would love for you to say no to Jesus but since you're not going to do that, he will be content if you say nothing at all. Don't dismiss confession as an empty religious work. True confession is one of the ways we reveal the good news of God's grace to a world that needs to hear it:

> Consequently, faith comes from hearing the message, and the message is heard through the word about Christ. But I ask: Did they not hear? Of course they did: "Their voice has gone out into all the earth, their words to the ends of the world." (Romans 10:17–18)

A word after

Early in the life of the blog, I picked up a reputation of being someone who is opposed to confession. Nothing could be further from the truth. (I also acquired a reputation for being someone who is opposed to repentance. Ditto.) What I am opposed to is the way confession has been used to enslave the children of the free.

After writing this article I heard from a man named David who was taught that one must confess every sin to be forgiven. David wanted to live righteously so he made it his habit to confess every sin. However, as a result of this belief he developed obsessive compulsive disorder (OCD, a.k.a. scrupulosity) and depression.

"No matter what I confessed, OCD would tell me I forgot something," said David. "I felt that I could not keep up with my sins, that I could literally spend my entire life confessing to God, and yet continue to suffer fear, guilt and self-condemnation."

After fifty years of living with OCD and depression, David found the gospel of grace and is now on his way to freedom. He still battles anxiety from time to time — half a century of living with an unhealthy mindset will do that to you — but he now understands that he is completely forgiven. "I now believe that complete forgiveness is included when you believe in Jesus, and is a gift we receive along with eternal life, righteousness, adoption as sons, acceptance, etc."

David's story is hardly unique. I have heard from many people who have developed mental illnesses because they thought they had to confess all their sins.

I write so that they might hear the good news of God's unconditional forgiveness and be free.

If your experience is like David's, I encourage you to define confession as the Bible does, as agreeing with God and proclaiming Jesus in our lives. What we put our minds to, determines what we feel. If you believe you must do things to earn forgiveness, you will feel the crippling weight of sin and obligation. However, if you believe you have been forgiven and that God loves you, is thoroughly pleased with you, and accepts you, you will be free.

10. Ten Myths about the Ministry of the Holy Spirit

Some people view the Holy Spirit as a kind of Divine Bookkeeper recording all their sins. But if Jesus did away with sin once and for all by the sacrifice of himself, what's left for the Holy Spirit to do? He must be unemployed!

In this article we're going to look at ten myths regarding the ministry of the Holy Spirit:

Myth 1: The Holy Spirit teaches me to keep the commandments
Truth 1: The Holy Spirit guides you into a relationship with Truth himself (John 16:13–14)

What did Jeremiah (31:33) mean when he prophesied that the Spirit would write his laws in our hearts? Was he promoting a relationship with the rules? No, Jesus is the law-keeper who lives within. Think of the Holy Spirit as a match-maker wooing you to Jesus. As we rest in Jesus and let him live his life through ours, we find ourselves keeping the commandments without any conscious effort.

Myth 2: The Holy Spirit is like a Divine Policeman enforcing law and order
Truth 2: The Holy Spirit strengthens and encourages the church (Acts 9:31)

Since many believers have been brought up on a diet of law and obligation, it is natural to think of the Holy Spirit as a Policeman enforcing God's commands. But this is confusing covenants. How does the Holy Spirit strengthen and build up the church? By revealing more and more of Jesus. The Holy Spirit is so good at what he does, that Jesus said that it was for our good that he leave so the Spirit could come (John 16:7). Think about that. We're better off now with the Spirit than we were with Jesus in the flesh.

Myth 3: The Holy Spirit is unpredictable, sort of the solo agent of heaven
Truth 3: The Holy Spirit speaks the words of the Father and the Son (Matthew 10:20, John 14:26)

They really are on the same team.

Myth 4: The Holy Spirit is mysterious and secretive—he's hard to figure out
Truth 4: The Holy Spirit gives us wisdom and revelation (Ephesians 1:17)

Jesus said the Holy Spirit would guide us into *all* truth, not some truth. He is not the author of confusion but the One who helps us make sense out of all Jesus said and did and everything that is about to happen (John 16:13, MSG). He really is the most wonderful Guide. Keep in step with the Spirit and you'll never put a foot wrong.

Myth 5: The Holy Spirit is scary
Truth 5: The Holy Spirit releases rivers of peace and joy (Romans 14:17)

Jesus said the Spirit would be in us like a river (John 7:38). Just as a river needs to flow, so does the Holy Spirit desire to flow out of you to refresh and bring life to others. One emotion which is consistently linked with the Holy Spirit is joy (e.g., Acts 13:52). If there is no joy in your walk, lean on the Holy Spirit. Believe that he is with you and in you to strengthen you with the Lord's joy.

Myth 6: The Holy Spirit is in the background somewhere — I'm not sure what he's up to
Truth 6: The Holy Spirit actively partners with us and empowers us to be bold witnesses (Acts 1:8)

In Greek the Holy Spirit is described as a *paraclete* (see John 16:7). The image is of a soldier who partners with us side-by-side in combat. And what a Powerful Partner he is! He never loses, he bears no scars, and his enemies have already been defeated. If you are saved then you already are acquainted with his work, for you could never have confessed Jesus as Lord without his help (1 Corinthians 12:3).

Many Christians know what it is to walk in the authority of Jesus' Name, but they do not fully operate in the power of the Spirit. They're like a cop with a badge and no gun. When the Spirit came on Saul in the Old Testament, the Bible says he was turned into another man who was empowered to do "whatever the occasion demands" (1 Samuel 10:6–7, NKJV). Similarly, in the new covenant the Spirit turns you into a new creation who is empowered to preach and demonstrate the gospel of the kingdom (1 Corinthians 2:4). This includes healing the sick, driving out demons, and raising the dead, as the occasion demands (Matthew 10:8).

Myth 7: The Holy Spirit leaves me speechless and anxious

Truth 7: The Holy Spirit gives you words to say so you need not worry (Mark 13:11)

Do you have an opportunity to speak but are stuck for words? Never fear for the gospel message is conveyed with words and wonders and the Holy Spirit provides them both. Trust him and ask for his wisdom. He gives generously and his words come packaged with boldness (Acts 4:31).

Myth 8: The Holy Spirit is a euphemism for the warm fuzzies I experience in the mood music after the preaching

Truth 8: The Holy Spirit reinforces the preaching of the gospel with signs and wonders (1 Thessalonians 1:5)

Some have diminished the role of the Holy Spirit to accommodate their limited experience of the supernatural, but Jesus promised that "signs will accompany those who believe" (Mark 16:17). What miracles were attributed to the Holy Spirit in the book of Acts? All of them! It's the book of *his* acts.

Every time the good news is preached, the Holy Spirit will look to confirm the message with signs following. His ministry is revealed in a Show and Tell gospel. "With that, Peter, full of the Holy Spirit, let loose…" (Acts 4:8, MSG). Cool, huh?

Myth 9: The Holy Spirit crushes me with impossible demands — he teaches me how to die daily

Truth 9: The Holy Spirit raises the dead, makes us new, gives life, warns us of dangers, and frees us from the burdens of manmade religion (Romans 8:11, Titus 3:5, Acts 20:23)

The ministry of the law brings death and condemnation, but the ministry of the Spirit brings life and righteousness (2 Corinthians 3:6–9). True, he'll let us come to the end of ourselves so that we might learn to trust him. But he loves you just the same whether you stay in the boat or dance upon the water. He comforts; he doesn't condemn.

Jesus promised us life in abundance (John 10:10). The Holy Spirit delivers on that promise by replacing fear with courage, weakness with strength, and death with resurrection life.

Myth 10: The Holy Spirit gives different groups different revelation which is why we have different denominations
Truth 10: The Holy Spirit baptizes us into one body (1 Corinthians 12:13)

There is one body, one Spirit, one hope, one Lord, one faith, one baptism, one God and Father of all, who is over all (Ephesians 4:4–6). We see the differences, but God sees one body with many members. God gives diverse gifts for a common purpose—that we might mature and reach unity in the faith. The Holy Spirit produces unity in the body, not division.

A word after

This article came out when E2R was about a year old. It didn't change the world or revolutionize the church, but it did prompt this comment from a man called Peter: "Paul, I've been receiving your writings for about six months. Your message deserves a wider audience. You should write a book."

Peter was one of several people who were saying the same thing at that time. I was initially dismissive. I wrote back, "Hi Peter, a few people have suggested I write a book, but why would anyone pay for something they can get for free."

Now I know better. Some people prefer books to blogs. People like yourself, for example.

11. What is Holiness? (It's Better Than You Think)

Holiness is avoiding sin. It's being set apart from the world and staying undefiled. Or so we've been told. The problem with defining holiness like this is that it doesn't actually describe a God who is holy. God was holy long before there was any sin to avoid. He was unblemished before there were blemishes.

In another article I looked at seven fairly useless definitions of holiness. All of them have a measure of truth but none of them contains the whole truth. None of them actually tells us what holiness is. And this is a problem because we are called to be holy. How can we be holy if we don't know what that means?

So what is holiness?

Holiness means wholeness. To say that "God is holy" is to refer the wholeness, fullness, beauty, and abundant life that overflows within the Godhead. God lacks nothing. He is unbroken, undamaged, unfallen, completely complete and entire within himself. He is the indivisible One, wholly self-sufficient, and the picture of perfection.

Holiness is not one aspect of God's character; it is the whole package in glorious unity. This is how Spurgeon describes it in his discourse on Psalm 99:5:

71

> Holiness is the harmony of all the virtues. The
> Lord has not one glorious attribute alone, or in
> excess, but all glories are in him as a whole; this is
> the crown of his honor and the honor of his
> crown.[1]

Holiness means perfection in the sense of completion.
When Jesus exhorts us to "be perfect" (Matthew 5:48),
he is inviting us to a life of wholeness and holiness.
The Greek word for "perfect" means "complete" or
"whole." Jesus was saying, "Be whole as your Father
in heaven is whole." Jesus came to make broken
people whole. He is calling us to the life that is his.

A holy and whole God stands in contrast to an
unholy and broken world. Because of sin and
separation we live in a world of death and scarcity. In
our natural state we are consumed with our needs
and lack. We spend our lives trying to get what we
don't have and trying to repair the damage of our
estrangement. But the only cure for our brokenness is
a revelation of a whole and holy God who lacks
nothing and who has promised to supply all our
needs out of his overflowing sufficiency.

We are to worship God in the beauty of his
holiness, yet much of what passes for worship is

---

[1] C. H. Spurgeon, *The Treasury of David*, "Psalm 99," The Spurgeon
Archive, 1885, website: www.spurgeon.org/treasury/ps099.htm,
(accessed November 7, 2014).

nothing more than grizzling about our ugliness. To the degree that we are conscious of our needs over his provision, we miss it. We don't understand all that Christ accomplished on our behalf.

The Bible declares we were sanctified (1 Corinthians 6:11); we have been made holy through his sacrifice and perfected forever (Hebrews 10:10,14); and we are complete in Christ (Colossians 2:10). In him we lack absolutely nothing. Yet we run here and there trying to gain what we already possess and speaking the faithless language of lack and longing.

We need to change our vocabulary. We need to start walking in our true identity of holiness. We need to thank him for who he is and what he's done. Here is a simple idea to help you do that. Whenever you read the words "holy" or "sanctified" in scripture, replace them with the heavenly language of wholeness and completion. This will give you a clearer insight into what Jesus has accomplished. Here are some examples:

To the church of God… to those *complete* in Christ Jesus and called to be *whole*. (1 Corinthians 1:2)

Put on the new self, created to be like God in true righteousness and *wholeness*. (Ephesians 4:24)

So do not be ashamed to testify about our Lord…
who has saved us and called us to a *whole and
complete* life — not because of anything we have
done but because of his own purpose and grace.
(2 Timothy 1:8–9)

But you are a chosen people, a royal priesthood, a
whole nation, a people belonging to God.
(1 Peter 2:9)

Jesus gives us a picture of a whole and holy life,
unbroken and unstained by sin. Everything Jesus
does is prefaced by holiness. His is a holy love, a holy
righteousness, a holy joy. Holiness, or wholeness, is
the very definition of abundant life. Such is the life
you already have in him.

A word after

This article triggered three questions among E2R
readers. Question #1: "I never heard of holiness being
defined as wholeness. Where did you get this
definition from?" Answer: the dictionary. At least, an
old dictionary.

At the time the Bible was first translated into
English, the word holy literally meant whole. You can
see this in old sermons where preachers used the

words holiness and wholeness interchangeably. For instance, Spurgeon in his note on Psalm 103:1, says:

> It is instructive to note how the Psalmist dwells upon the holy name of God, as if his holiness were dearest to him; or, perhaps, because the holiness or wholeness of God was to his mind the grandest motive for rendering to him the homage of his nature in its wholeness.[2]

Substitute the word holy for wholly or whole in the New Testament, and you'll see that it fits perfectly.

Question #2: "Why do the New Testament writers call us to be holy (e.g., 1 Peter 1:15)? How do we read these exhortations through the lens of grace?" Some holiness preachers interpret New Testament exhortations as guidelines on how to make yourself holy, but trust me, you can't do it. God's standards are too high. Only grace can save a sinner and make a broken person whole (or holy).

The same New Testament writers who exhort us to be holy tell us in many places that we are already holy in Christ (e.g., 1 Peter 2:9). So the only way to interpret "Be holy" is in the sense of "Be who you are and stop acting otherwise." Christians who act

---

[2] C. H. Spurgeon, *The Treasury of David*, "Psalm 103," The Spurgeon Archive, 1885, website: www.spurgeon.org/treasury/ps103.htm, (accessed November 7, 2014).

unholy are acting contrary to their new nature in Christ.

Question #3: "Won't this message just produce complacency? If we are positionally holy in this fallen world, shouldn't we strive to become totally holy?"

The notion that there are positional truths which are distinct from real truths is dangerous and unbiblical. When we were sinners we weren't *positionally* sinners — we were bona fide sinners. Now that we are in Christ we are genuinely righteous and holy. Your holiness isn't merely positional; it's as real as it gets. If you are one with the Lord you are as righteous and holy as he is (see 1 John 4:17). That's a fact.

We don't act holy to become holy. We act holy because, in Christ, we *are* holy. It's who we truly are.

12. Twelve Famous Examples of
Walking in the Spirit

The Bible describes two kinds of life and two ways to live. You are either *in the flesh* or *in the spirit* (Romans 8:9), and you will either walk *according to the flesh* or *according to the spirit* (Galatians 5:25). The unbeliever lives in the flesh and walks according to the flesh. The Christian is in the spirit and ideally walks after the spirit. Yet the Bible provides many examples of saints who walked after the flesh. In Galatia there was an entire church that did so.

Walking after the old ways of the flesh is abnormal for a believer. It's like a butterfly who acts as though he was still a caterpillar. Walking after the flesh is walking by sight. It's doing what seems right in your own eyes and leaning on your own understanding. It's trusting your own judgment and ignoring the Holy Spirit.

What does it mean to walk after the spirit? It's walking by faith. It's being mindful of what God has said and is now saying and what God has done and is now doing. Are there any examples of this in the Bible? There are plenty. Pick anything Jesus did and you will see a man who consistently walked according to the spirit. Jesus is our best model of a life lived in step with the Holy Spirit.

But Jesus was not the only one who walked in the spirit. This way of life was normal for many New Testament believers. However, in my list of twelve examples below, I have taken care to pick stories where the Bible clearly indicates that an individual was walking in the spirit.

This list gives us a picture of how life is meant to be for a Christian. It is a picture of the abundant life that Jesus promised to us. It portrays the kind of life that I wish to live.

1. Simeon has a date with destiny. For hundreds of years the prophets had been straining to see the promised Messiah, then Simeon, "moved by the Holy Spirit," goes to the temple courts and sees what all the others missed (Luke 2:27). Talk about all your Christmasses coming at once! Those who are led by the Spirit are always at the right place at the right time.

2. Jesus lives free. He shunned labels, refused to be controlled, and ate with whomever he pleased. Friends tried to manage him, powerful men tried to control him, and Satan tried to tempt him. But Jesus stayed free of their unholy influence because his eyes were on his Father. He was not distracted by success or apparent failure and he could sleep through storms. Because he was secure in his sonship he remained totally free.

3. Jesus is the life of the party. At the wedding in Capernaum Jesus didn't think his time had come, but Mary and the Holy Spirit had other ideas (see John 2:4). The kingdom of heaven is a party (Matthew 22:2) and those who are led by the Spirit are the life of that heavenly party wherever they go.

4. Jesus heals all the sick (Matthew 12:15, 14:36). In his flesh Jesus could not heal a headache any more than you could. Walking in the spirit you can heal the sick, just as Jesus did.

5. Jesus delivers all who are oppressed by the devil (Acts 10:38). He drove out demons with a word (Matthew 8:16). No spooky exorcisms or long-drawn out altar calls—just a word of irresistible authority backed up by the most powerful being in the universe: the Holy Spirit.

6. Jesus teaches with authority (Matthew 7:29). In contrast with those who minister condemnation by teaching rules, those who are led by the spirit speak words of eternal life (John 6:68). In contrast with those who preach paralyzing homilies of uncertainty, those led by the spirit declare truth with unshakeable conviction. Jesus didn't try to grow his ministry and he didn't run after crowds. Crowds ran after him.

7. Peter and John declare the gospel boldly in the face of persecution (Acts 4:8). The Holy Spirit still emboldens "unschooled and ordinary" men.

8. Stephen refutes the legalistic arguments of religious trouble-makers (Acts 6:10). Those who serve in the newness of the spirit will encounter opposition from those who persist in the oldness of the letter. There may even be persecution (just ask Stephen, Peter, Paul, James, etc.). But no weapon formed against you will prosper and you will refute every judgmental and critical tongue that rises in opposition to the message of Christ and his finished work.

9. Barnabas sees potential in Paul (Acts 9:27). None of the apostles trusted the man once known as Saul, but Barnabas saw what no one else saw and through one act of encouragement changed the course of history.

10. Paul writes about a new covenant. Jesus revealed the grace of God and Paul wrote it down so we wouldn't forget. With "words taught by the Spirit" Paul preached a message that went against everything he had learned in Pharisee school (1 Corinthians 2:13). In the natural Paul was unqualified—his old training was useless and

dung-like. But those who minister in the new covenant of the spirit have a "competence that comes from God" (2 Corinthians 3:6).

11. Paul goes to Macedonia instead of Bithynia (Acts 16:7). As a result, the Philippians got the gospel and we got the most joy-filled letter in the Bible. Those who walk after the spirit know that God's plans are always better than the ones we make ourselves.

12. Paul finishes his race in style. While serving time on death row, Paul wrote words that have been etched on countless headstones:

> I have fought the good fight, I have finished the race, I have kept the faith. Now there is in store for me the crown of righteousness, which the Lord, the righteous Judge, will award to me on that day. (2 Timothy 4:7–8a)

In the last line of his last letter, this spirit-conscious apostle reminds us of the secret of living well: "The Lord Jesus Christ is with thy spirit... Amen" (2 Timothy 4:22, YLT).

A word after

In my original E2R article I said that Paul was led by the spirit to go to Jerusalem. I may have gotten that one wrong (which is why I edited it out above). The King James Bible said Paul "purposed in the spirit" to go meaning he decided to go (Acts 19:21). But an unusual meeting with a prophet in Caesarea suggests that the Holy Spirit didn't want him to go (Acts 21:10–11). Not only that, but spirit-filled believers in two towns pleaded with Paul to steer clear of Jerusalem (Acts 21:4, 12). However, Paul ignored them all and went anyway triggering a train of events that resulted in him being taken to Rome in chains.

Why did Paul go to Jerusalem despite the warnings of the Holy Spirit and his friends? Maybe he was weary of traveling and wanted to come "home" to Jerusalem. Or maybe he was looking to die as a martyr. "I am ready not only to be bound, but also to die in Jerusalem for the name of the Lord Jesus" (Acts 21:13). Whatever his motives, Paul seems to have convinced himself, at least initially, that he was "compelled by the Spirit" to go (Acts 20:22).

13. Does God Use Correction Fluid?

Is your name written in the Lamb's Book of Life? Are you worried that Jesus may blot out your name? It seems that many believers are. They are afraid that they may do something that will cause Jesus to blot out their names. It's like Jesus is sitting in heaven with a pen in one hand and a bottle of correction fluid in the other. Get saved, name goes in. Fail a test, name goes out. Recommit your life to God, name goes back in. Phew! With all the recommitments going on, you'd think Jesus was in danger of repetitive stress injury!

But seriously, do you fear that Jesus might remove your name from his book? Is this something that concerns you?

> Anyone whose name was not found written in the Book of Life was thrown into the lake of fire. (Revelation 20:15)

Whatever the Book of Life is, it seems important that your name is found in it. But if your name is already recorded, should you be worried about being blotted out? Under the old covenant, the answer seemed to be yes:

The Lord replied to Moses, "Whoever has sinned against me I will blot out of my book." (Exodus 32:33)

Under the old covenant, your performance mattered a great deal. You were blessed if you were faithful, but condemned if you weren't. This meant people were very conscious of their behavior. They knew that their sinful behavior could lead to dire consequences.

But we don't live under that old sin-conscious covenant. We live under the new and better covenant of God's grace. Under grace, your performance affects your standing before God not one bit. Jesus did it all. We are not blessed because we are faithful but because *he* is faithful.

Mixing covenants

So why are believers worried that Jesus will blot their names out of his book? Their fear stems from an old covenant interpretation of a new covenant promise. I am referring to the exhortation Jesus' gave to the church in Sardis:

He who overcomes shall be clothed in white garments, and I will not blot out his name from the Book of Life… (Revelation 3:5a, NKJV)

Here Jesus gives us a wonderful assurance of our eternal salvation. He is promising that he will never blot out our names. Never means never!

Yet some read this as if Jesus might do the very thing he promised not to do. Someone with an old covenant mindset looks at this verse and sees only conditions for salvation. They think, "I have to overcome to qualify. If I don't overcome, I'm going to be blotted out."

But read this verse with a new covenant mindset and you'll see it in a completely different way. You'll think, "Jesus has overcome the world and now lives in me. I don't overcome to qualify — I am qualified by Christ and I carry his overcoming nature. This is not some test I have to pass, but a wonderful promise regarding my inheritance" (see 1 John 4:4, 5:5 and John 16:33).

God has perfect knowledge. When he added your name to his book he knew everything you had done and everything you would ever do. There is nothing you can do that would cause him to shake his head with disappointment and say, "I made a mistake adopting that one." God doesn't make mistakes. When he added you to his book it was for all eternity.

There's only one thing God promises to blot out, and it's not your name — it's your sins:

> I, even I, am he who blots out your transgressions,
> for my own sake, and remembers your sins no
> more. (Isaiah 43:25)

God promised to blot out all your sins and he did that
already. This was the new thing foretold in Isaiah
43:19. Under the old covenant, men's sins were
counted against them. But when Jesus met all the
demands of the law at the cross, all your sins were
blotted out. Why did he blot out your sins? He did it
because he loves us and so that we might be
reconciled to him.

If your name is in his book, you have nothing to
fear on Judgment Day. If all your sins were blotted
out at the cross, then there is no sin left that could get
your name removed from his book. This is the gospel
of grace. It was new news for Isaiah, is old news for
us, but is still good news for everyone.

A word after

This article was the first of many I have since written
on the subject of eternal security and it attracted
criticism from those who worry I am giving false
assurance to Christians. One critic wrote that I was
"dangerous to the faith" and gave me lots of scriptures to prove that Jesus might do the very thing he
promised not to do. Another asked, "Are you sure?"

as in, "Are you sure that Jesus won't blot out our names?"

The "are you sure" question stirs me because I have found that my confidence on matters of grace repels some people. Apparently it's not politically correct to *be sure*. After all, the "I'm right, you're wrong" attitude of religious dogma has given rise to some of history's worst atrocities. It's far better, according to some, to be open-minded and *un*sure. Only by being open to a buffet of beliefs can we be sure that we aren't deluding ourselves

I'm not so sure.

Life is full of uncertainty and there are many things we can't be sure about. But surely we can be sure about the goodness of God and his intentions towards us. Isn't that the whole point of the cross? In a world full of questions, the cross is an exclamation mark. In a world full of half-truths and lies, Jesus is *the* Truth. He's the Rock on which we stand.

It is my conviction that the enemy wants us to be either opposed to God's grace or uncertain about it. He would prefer you to be an unbeliever, but if you must be a believer, then be an *unbelieving* believer. Be one of those double-minded folk who glorify questions that lead nowhere and who worship at the altar of uncertainty. Be someone who is slow of heart to believe God's word.

Not me. I want to be like Dr. Luke who began his gospel account one with these words:

> With this in mind, since I myself have carefully investigated everything from the beginning, I too decided to write an orderly account for you, most excellent Theophilus, *so that you may know the certainty of the things you have been taught.* (Luke 1:3–4, emphasis added)

Luke wanted his readers to be certain and so do I, because certainty is the essence of faith. "Faith is being certain…" (Hebrews 11:1). It's being persuaded about God and his promises.

Am I sure Jesus won't blot out our names? I'm as sure as I am about anything that God has promised. In other words, I am *very* sure. You can be too.

14. Take Up Your Cross Daily

Jesus said, "Whoever wants to be my disciple must deny themselves and take up their cross daily and follow me" (Luke 9:23). What does it mean to take up your cross daily? I'm going to give you two interpretations and then you can choose.

Interpretation #1: Jesus is preaching self-denial

Following Christ is all about self-denial and going without. If you are not in the daily habit of denying your appetites and desires, you are not a real Christian. The more you deny your own needs and wants, the holier you'll be. So fast every day, give until it hurts, and you'll be just like Jesus.

But there's a problem with this interpretation. Abstaining from food, Facebook, or fun won't make you righteous and holy. This message of self-denial is nothing more than the ancient practice of asceticism dressed up in religious jargon. It is a message that promotes Pharisaical self-righteousness and DIY Christianity.

Another problem is that this message will leave you anxious and insecure. "Have I denied myself enough?" You can never know. So you'd better deny yourself some more, just to be safe. "Don't touch, don't handle, don't taste." Pretty soon you'll be whipping yourself and asking your friends to crucify you for the Easter parade.

Pshaw! Jesus did not suffer and die on the cross so you could join him in suffering and dying on a cross as well. That's not good news. Jesus died so that we might be free from this sort of dead and useless religion.

Interpretation #2: Jesus is showing us the way to salvation

And who is the way? Jesus. When Jesus says, "Follow me," he's saying the way to salvation is through him and his cross. As Paul said, "I have been crucified with Christ and I no longer live, but Christ lives in me…" (Galatians 2:20a).

The reason most Christians struggle to live the Christian life is that they do not know they have died with Christ. Yet Paul says so again and again. To the Christians in Colossae: "You died with Christ" (Colossians 2:20). To the believers in Rome: "We died with Christ" (Romans 6:8). To the Corinthians: "We died" (2 Corinthians 5:14).

When you were baptized or placed into Christ, you were baptized into his death (Romans 6:3). This may be the single most important thing that ever happened to you, yet many Christians are unaware of it. Since they don't know that they died, they are constantly trying to die. But the gospel declares, "You died."

You have been crucified with Christ. The person you used to be — dead in sins and alienated from the life of God — no longer lives, but Christ lives in you.

"But if I died with Christ, why does Jesus say we must take up our cross *daily*?"

First of all, note that the word daily is found only once in the three accounts of Jesus' words. Jesus said, "Whoever wants to be my disciple must deny themselves and …

...take up their cross and follow me." (Matthew 16:24)

...take up their cross and follow me." (Mark 8:34)

...take up their cross daily and follow me." (Luke 9:23)

Why does Luke record the word daily when Matthew and Mark do not? "Our English translations of Luke are wrong," says the venerable commentator Adam Clarke, "for the word daily is not in some of the original manuscripts."[3]

---

[3] Adam Clarke, *Commentary on the Whole Bible*, "Luke chapter 9," 1832, website: www.sacred-texts.com/bib/cmt/clarke/luk009.htm, (accessed November 7, 2014). What AC actually says is this: "Daily is omitted by many reputable MSS., versions, and fathers. It is not found in the parallel places, Mat 16:24; Mar 8:34."

Adam Clarke may be right. I wouldn't know, I don't have the original manuscripts. But for the sake of argument, let's assume Mr. Clarke is wrong and our English Bibles have it right. What then?

Why does Luke say "daily"?

Luke isn't contradicting Matthew and Mark; he's saying the same thing but with gusto. He's saying we ought to value the finished work of the cross every day.

When I get out of bed in the morning and put my feet on the floor, my left foot says, "Thank you, Jesus," and my right foot says, "For the cross." It's because you have died with Christ that you now live, everyday, in union with him. This is a great treasure and not something to take for granted.

"Paul, are you saying that if I stop valuing the cross I'll lose my salvation?" Not at all. I'm saying if you have been born of the spirit, learn to walk by the spirit. We don't die daily — once will do the trick — and we don't get born again, again and again. But every day we make this choice: Will I walk after the old way of the flesh or the new way of the spirit?

Let me give you an example. Say you hear a message that says you need to fast and pray to become spiritually mature, so you decide to fast and pray. Bam! You are no longer walking after the spirit.

You are no longer trusting in the grace of God. You are trusting in your own fasting and praying performance. Where does the Lord fit in this picture? He doesn't and that's the problem. DIY religion is a graceless and faithless way to live.

Walking after the flesh doesn't necessarily mean running around getting drunk and doing bad stuff. For the moral person, the flesh takes on the subtler guise of good works, duty, and self-improvement. These good things are harmful to the extent that they encourage us to rely on the flesh — our resources, understanding, and ability — instead of trusting in Jesus.

What does it mean to die to self?

There is nothing wrong with the phrase "die to self." The problem comes when we read it through religious lenses instead of gospel lenses. We think, "I have to stop being who God made me to be. I have to pretend I'm somebody else — someone who doesn't enjoy wine, one woman, and song." That's a dehumanizing doctrine of demons.

God made you unique. He gave you dreams and desires that no one else has. When you suppress your God-given dreams and desires, the world is impoverished.

Die to self means trust Jesus and distrust self. It means live each day out of the glorious relationship you have with the Lord. It means don't fall back to the inferior ways of the flesh that you once walked in, but stand firm in the freedom of Christ.

This, I believe, is the point Luke was trying to make. The trusting life is an adventure. It's good to remind yourself daily that "God is for me. How can I fail?" Conscious of your loving Father's acceptance and approval, you will soar on eagles' wings. And when you apprehend the inexhaustible riches of his grace, the whole world benefits.

Why would you want to waste one single day living any other way? Why crawl when you can fly?

A word after

A reader from the Philippines asked me, "Is it wrong to fast?" Not at all. Have the freedom to fast and have the freedom to fast from fasting. But if you do fast, be clear about the reason *why* you are fasting. Fasting won't make you righteous and holy and it won't cause God to bless you. He's already given you every blessing in Christ.

Based on Christ's words in Matthew 17:21, some say that fasting helps to starve the flesh and defeat natural unbelief. Maybe that's so, but I think a revelation of Jesus is the best cure for unbelief.

Jesus said two things about fasting that are interesting. He said any fasting should be done in secret (Matthew 6:6–18), and that his disciples wouldn't fast for as long he was with them. "How can the guests of the bridegroom fast while he is with them?" (Mark 2:19). Any fasting would take place when the bridegroom was taken away and I guess that's what happened when Jesus was taken to be tortured and crucified. That was a tough time for the disciples and I imagine they didn't eat.

But Jesus said he would return and make his home with us and he's done that with his Holy Spirit. Do you see? The bridegroom is with us. This is not the time to mourn but to celebrate and rejoice. Do happy men fast?

There's more to say about this but I'll leave you with some quick final thoughts: I'm fasting from the law. I'm fasting from the tree of knowledge of good and evil. I'm fasting from all those self-righteous attitudes and habits I used to think made me a better person.

I'm feasting on Jesus.

15. The Other Reason for the Season

How did Mary get to Bethlehem? If you get your history from Christmas cards, you might think that she rode on a donkey. But it is unlikely that Joseph owned a donkey. Joseph was poor—he brought a poor man's offering of two doves when they presented baby Jesus in the temple (see Luke 2:24 and Leviticus 5:7). In those days, a donkey was such a treasured possession that coveting one was expressly forbidden in the Ten Commandments (Exodus 20:17).

Joseph could neither afford a decent place to stay or a lamb for the sacrifice, so the odds are that he didn't own a donkey. So how did Mary travel from Nazareth to Bethlehem, a distance of about 80 miles? She probably walked.

Right there all the mothers reading this just winced. *She walked 80 miles pregnant? Trust a man to leave an important detail like that out of his account.* To be fair to Luke and the other gospel writers, we don't know exactly how Mary got to Bethlehem. But I have a theory—a Christmas tale if you like—and it begins with some good news…

The Gospel of Gabriel

Mary's life was radically changed when an angel uttered the following words to her: "Greetings, you who are highly favored! The Lord is with you" (Luke 1:28).

At first Mary was troubled. I wouldn't say it was disbelief so much as sheer incomprehension. "How can this be?"

The favor of God is mind-boggling. Our minds cannot explain it. Happily, you don't need to explain it to receive it. You just have to believe and Mary did.

"May it be to me as you have said" (Luke 1:38). Right there is faith. The grace-faith circuit complete, favor now begins to flow from heaven to Mary. Then the angel left.

Did you know that only two people in the Bible were regarded as *highly* favored? One of them is Mary, the other one is you. "He made us accepted (literally, *highly favored*) in the Beloved" (Ephesians 1:6).

To the degree that Mary was favored, so are you. It's perfectly fine to put Mary on a favor pedestal as long as you put yourself right up there too.

It is significant that the angel did not leave until Mary responded in faith. God's favor was on her but she needed to believe it to receive it. So do you.

You need to cultivate the habit of seeing yourself as God sees you—as highly favored and deeply loved.

Mary's mystery marathon

So how did Mary get to Bethlehem? I can't prove it, but I suspect a miracle took place. Perhaps it was something like what God did when he brought the Israelites out of slavery:

> You yourselves have seen what I did to Egypt, and how I carried you on eagles' wings and brought you to myself. (Exodus 19:4)

No, I don't think Mary and Joseph hitched a ride on real eagles—this isn't *The Lord of the Rings*. When God says he carried them on eagle's wings he's saying "I brought you to myself swiftly and easily."

My hunch is that Mary and Joseph walked effortlessly and without trouble. They journeyed under a hot Middle Eastern sun without fainting or growing weary because God "gives strength to the weary and increases the power of the weak" (Isaiah 40:29). When it came time to deliver history's most famous baby, Mary wasn't worn out from completing back-to-back marathons. She was full of life and the picture of health.

At least that's how she looks on the Christmas cards.

Bethlehem means "the house of bread." At the house of bread Mary and Joseph came face-to-face with the Bread of Life. In a sense, God had brought them to himself for it was in Bethlehem that they first laid eyes on their Savior Jesus.

What relevance does Mary's journey have for us today?

Mary's journey is the same journey you made when you got saved. When you got born again, you walked on Mary's Trail. Think about it. Some angel or messenger told you the good news of God's favor, you wondered "how can this be?" and then after some time you came face to face with the Bread of Life. You met Jesus and got born again. Like Mary, you may have travelled a long road, but the journey itself was miraculous. Egypt is in your past because God has brought you to himself on eagle's wings.

The other reason for the season

Christmas is not just the time when we celebrate Jesus' arrival into the world. It's also the time when we celebrate his arrival into *our* world. Grace came 2000 years ago but it meant nothing until the day we believed it and got born again. So in a way, it's not just his birthday we're celebrating, it's our birthday too.

This Christmas, as much of the world gathers around the manger in adoration, why not take a moment to reflect on your journey to the House of

Bread. Jesus is the reason for the season but ask yourself this: Why did he come? He came to save you. In his eyes you are the pearl of great price and the treasure in the field. As far as Jesus is concerned, *you* are the reason for the season.

You are highly favored and deeply loved! Oh Happy Day! Oh Happy Christmas!

A word after

After reading this article a reader asked me whether it's a sin to celebrate Christmas. "I watched a YouTube video which confused me by saying Christmas is a pagan holiday and the Lord is against it. I'm really confused now."

It is not a sin to celebrate Jesus' birth! I am aware that some people seem to delight in finding the evil in everything, even Christmas, but Paul wrote, "To the pure, all things are pure" (Titus 1:15).

Do not let anyone judge you… with regard to a religious festival, a New Moon celebration or a Sabbath day. These are a shadow of the things that were to come; the reality, however, is found in Christ. (Colossians 2:16–17)

Christmas is the shadow; Jesus is the reality. Christmas comes alive when we do it in honor of

Jesus, when we remember who he is and why he came. Christmas is about Jesus coming for you with love in his eyes and healing in his hands. Surely that is something to celebrate!

If you enjoyed this book, why not subscribe to E2R and get more articles just like these sent to your email. It's free! Sign up at:

escapetoreality.org/subscribe

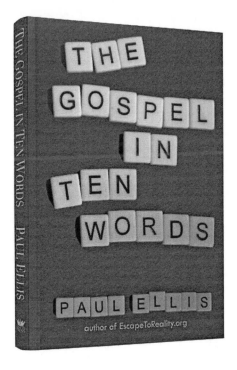

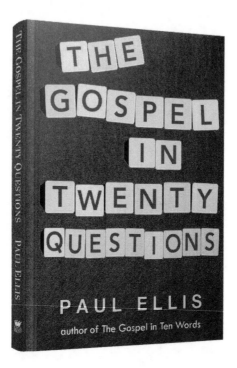

Printed in Great Britain
by Amazon.co.uk, Ltd.,
Marston Gate.